#WORDMAN

Word

Man

By: Dr. Perry

PetitePsy.D

Last remarks By: Dr. Shay

PetitePsy.D

Disclaimer

Printed in the United States of America. All rights reserved. No part of this publication may be reproduced, stored in or introduced into a retrieval system, or transmitted, in any form, or by any means (electronic, mechanical, photocopying, recording or otherwise) without prior permission of the publisher. Any person who does any unauthorized act in relation to this publication may be liable to criminal prosecution and civil claims for damages. All scripture quotations, unless otherwise indicated are taken from the

New King James Version of the Bible Copyright © 1982 by Thomas Nelson, Inc. used by permission. All rights reserved.

Dedication

I would like to start with this statement. You already know, JESUS A THOUSAND TIMES! ANYTHING ELSE WOULD BE UNCIVILIZED. MY wife Shawanda Le'chea Petite who often time wouldn't let me set doing nothing but knowing the gift in me and coupled with the Word she continues to push me. My Pops and Nana David and Wanda Oatis who when I need direction, discipline and even a place to live it was through them the Lord provided. My family Percy Petite, Serena Harris, Kenneth Petite, Carolyn Petite, and Audrey Petite (my sister in heaven) who never stop believing God for me and in me. My father and mother Joe L. Wilson and Veatter Clayton who God used to get me in to the Earth for his purpose and glory. I love all of you and we all will both learn to be more conscious of our words to manifest heaven on Earth by what we say!

Contents

Disclaimer	2
Dedication	4
Foreword	7
Introduction	8
Chapter1 **Word**	15
Chapter2 **The Tongue**	22
Chapter3 **Team Work**	46
Chapter4 **Be Slow To Speak**	53
Chapter5 **Word And Flesh**	60
Chapter6 **Word And Spirit**	64
Last Remarks	73

Foreword

The book Word Man is just what it says. Word is not some lifeless force that moves about in the world, yet rather it's a force of Life, meaning that it's full of this Life and is able to reproduce this Life. One must be willing to position themselves to know and understand the Life of Word man. This man in essence is the words of a statement that is now active of the fulfillment of itself. (What is Word man working of for you?) Because just as sure as you said it it's coming to pass.

Word man functions just as the body, as the body is made up of many members, Word man functions just as the body, as the body is made up of many members. Word man is made up of many words all working together to achieve a common goal and ultimate process.

Introduction

The purpose of this book is to make you, (the reader) the believer, or even the unbeliever conscious of the *word* you release from your mouth. The goal is to change your perspective, your mindset, your outlook concerning *word* and ultimately the way you use them.

When *word* is released from your lips, before it can get a foot away from your mouth you NEED to see it take the form of a living being or even as a man. You MUST see the *word* take form and become as an active unstoppable force. You need to know that once *word* takes this form it is on a mission. As a man on a mission with tunnel vision, focused only on doing what he has been purposed to do, this is what happens with *word*.

ONCE *WORD* IS RELEASED IT'S ALSO ACTIVATED!

Word is SELFISH and SELF-SEEKING and SELF-FULFILLING!

When I say that *word* is selfish, I mean it is DEVOTED to or caring only for itself; it has concern primarily with its own interest, benefits, and welfare regardless of others.

When I say that *word* is self-seeking, "I am saying that it selfishly advances to its own end."

The Bible also describes *word* as self-fulfilling, meaning what is spoken happens or is brought about as a result of being foretold, expected or talked about.

Isaiah 61:11(Amp) says "For as [surely as] the earth brings forth its shoots, and as a garden causes what is sown in it to spring forth, so [surely] the Lord

God will cause rightness and justice and praise to spring forth before all the nations [through the self-fulfilling power of His word]."

Just as word went forth from the mouth of the Creator of the Earth in the Garden of Eden when God said in Genesis 3:15, "And I will put enmity between you and the woman, and between your offspring and her Offspring: He will bruise and tread your head underfoot, and you will lie in wait and bruise his heel."

From the very moment *word* was spoken from the mouth of God it took the form of a man walking with legs and having a mind, eyes, muscles and possessing a heart.

Word's legs begin to walk in the direction of the end result. The mind of *word* became focused on the completion of the mission. *Word's* eyes set its sight only on the target, blinded to anything else. *Word's* muscle, the strength of *word,* fought against all negative forces that would try to hinder the mission and *word's* heart, filled with passion to fulfill itself, was the driving force.

Word walked through 42 generations of men non-stop, fearless and focused on returning with the completion of itself.

God the Father used prophets in the Old Testament of the Bible as a reminder to man that this *word* had not died, failed, been forgotten, extinguished or aborted, but it would indeed produce what had been spoken. The *word* carried so much power that at the perfect time the *word* that was released and seemed invisible to the eye of man was made visible for all to see and the effects of its power was witnessed by many. This *word* that was spoken in the Garden of Eden walked through generations and produced Jesus of Nazareth who became the Savior of the world.

Still today *word* possesses this same power.

In Jeremiah Chapter 1, God put His *word* in Jeremiah's mouth because He needed a body in the earth realm to release the *word*. And God told Jeremiah that he would root out, pull down, destroy, over throw, build and plant and all these things would be accomplished with *word*. Read the book of Jeremiah and see that Jeremiah NEVER did any of these things with his hands.

God also made it clear to Jeremiah what *word* he SHOULD NOT speak.

{But the Lord said to me, say not I am only a youth; for you shall go to all to whom I shall send you, and whatever I command you, you shall speak.} Jeremiah 1:7

With *word* you build your world and with *word* you tear down your world. With *word* you destroy things and with *word* you plant things.

It's vital that we understand *word*.

While *word* has life giving, creative, constructive and building power. *Word* also has the power to kill, destroy, destruct, and tear down.

With *word* ONLY Jesus put to death a fig tree that once had life.

With word ONLY Jesus spoke to the wind and waves and caused what once raged to be at peace.

With *word* alone you can tear down the self-esteem of those that love you. When we were children we were taught and we chanted, "Sticks and stones may break my bones but *words* will never hurt me."

After reading this book you will know that this chant was a lie from the pits of hail. I would venture to say that your *words* have more power to hurt you than any sticks or stones if you use *word* in the wrong way.

I pray that after this in depth look at *word* and its potential, that you will be conscious of how you use *word*. No longer throw *word* around frivolously but use it with purpose because once you release *word* what you have spoken is already done and you will have just what you have spoken because that *word* is formed, activated and on assignment to complete the mission. That *word* will selfishly advance to its own end. MANIFESTATION!!!!!

By:Kenya GreenPsy.D

Chapter 1

WORD

Word is the most powerful forces in the universe. It is by way of *Word* the universe has its existence. It is alive having the ability to produce, construct, tear down, and build up. *Word* is a creative force that is going to work for you or against you. In every *word* that is released from the mouth of a man(male man or female man) you can find this ability.

Hebrews 11:3 KJV

[3] Through faith we understand that the worlds were framed by the *word* of God, so that things

which are seen were not made of things which do appear.

Everything you see or don't see is a product of *word*. I know you are probably saying what is this *(word.) Word* is an unseen force like the wind. The wind is an unseen force that when it's on the move you don't see it but you see the results or effects of its existence. A friend of mine would ask a question,"When the trees would be swaying back and forth because of the moving of the wind, "Do you see that wind?"Because we always thought that's what it was.We would state, "Yes." and then he would state."That is not the wind, but it is the manifestation of the wind because the wind is unseen."

Word is the one thing that's able to grab that which is in the unseen realm and pull it into the seen realm making it visible for all eyes to see.

Romans 4:17 KJV

[17] ("As it is written, I have made thee a father of many nations,) before him whom he believed, even God, who quickeneth the dead, and calleth those things which be not as though they were."

Here I would like to point out a few thoughts.

- Looking at the later part of this verse we see, (calleth those things). This would be a clear indication that (those things) do exist in another realm. The unseen realm.

- Which be not:

- The idea here is that they(be not) or do not exist in the seen realm.
- As though they were: Here God call for those things that are in one realm to be in another. What is it that God uses to do this? *Word.*
- Here I would like to point out that word has the ability to operate in two realms. When you see in the *Word* of God, the blind given sight, the lame made to walk, the leapers cleansed, and the maim made whole:This is *word* in action in the seen realm.

Mark 3:5 KJV "And when he had looked round about on them with anger, being grieved for the hardness of their hearts, he saith unto the man, Stretch forth thine hand. And he stretched it out: and his hand was restored whole as the other."

Matthew 8:3 KJV "And Jesus put forth his hand, and touched him, saying, I will; be thou clean. And immediately his leprosy was cleansed."

Luke 5:24 KJV "But that ye may know that the Son of man hath power upon earth to forgive sins, (he said unto the sick of the palsy,) I say unto thee, Arise, and take up thy couch, and go into thine house."

John 5:8-9 KJV "Jesus saith unto him, Rise, take up thy bed, and walk. And immediately the man was made whole, and took up his bed, and walked: and on the same day was the sabbath."

When you see in the *Word* of God, devils being cast out, the dead raised to life, and a tree being dried up at the roots, this is *word* in action in the unseen realm.

John 11:43 KJV "And when he thus had spoken, he cried with a loud voice, Lazarus, come forth."

Mark 5:8 KJV "For he said unto him, Come out of the man, thou unclean spirit."

Luke 17:6 KJV "And the Lord said, If ye had faith as a grain of mustard seed, ye might say unto this sycamine tree, Be thou plucked up by the root, and be thou planted in the sea; and it should obey you."

I would like to point out some things in this last passage to better help us see this thought.

- Faith is the evidence of that which (IS), even though it is not seen.
- In order for it to get what you want done *(word)* must be present.
- The root of every tree is unseen because the roots are under the ground.

The thing that needs to be known about every scripture that is used is that they have this one thing in common.

(SOMETHING IS SAID)

Word has no existence apart from something being said.

Chapter 2

THE TONGUE

Proverbs 18:21 KJV

[21] Death and life are in the power of the tongue: and they that love it shall eat the fruit thereof.

Here's the thought, the world is a swimming pool and the tongue is the diving board. The power of any diving board is in its ability to spring forth or catapult one into the air. The power of the tongue is its ability to form *word*. *Word* springs forth as to be *catapult* from the tongue for a specific reason, purpose, aim, goal, and intent.

Definition of Catapult:

- A device in which accumulated tension is suddenly released.
- A military machine worked by a lever and ropes for launching large stones.
- To hurl or launch something in a specified direction.

The power of the tongue is accumulated tension with sudden release of every *word* man. The mouth is like a contraption/machine that power flows from, at the pull of the lever which is better known as the tongue, releasing that power in the form of *word*man. *Word* Man has a specified task with specified direction. Let's look at this *word* power in the Strong's dictionary.

Power (Hebrew-Yawd):

Synoptic words are:

Creative Ability

Direction

Remote

Because Of

Let me put these definitions in a sentence.

Because of the creative ability to remotely control our lives in the direction we desire with words we speak with purpose.

Because we are products of a word God, (John1:1), who created the worlds with His word, (Hebrews11:3) also upholding all things by the *word* of His power, (Hebrews 1:3), begot us by the word of truth. (James 1:18)

Let's take another look at the tongue from the book of James.

James 3:1-8 KJV "My brethren, be not many masters, knowing that we shall receive the greater condemnation. For in many things we offend all. If any man offend not in word, the same is a perfect man, and able also to bridle the whole body. Behold, we put bits in the horses' mouths, that they may obey us; and we turn about their whole body. Behold also the ships, which though they be so great, and are driven of fierce winds, yet are they turned about with a very small helm, whithersoever the governor listeth. Even so the tongue is a little member, and boasteth great things. Behold, how great a matter a little fire kindleth! And the tongue is a fire, a world of iniquity: so is the tongue among our members, that it defileth the whole body, and setteth on fire the course of nature; and it is set on fire of hell. For every kind of beasts, and of birds, and of serpents, and of things in the sea, is tamed, and hath been tamed of mankind: But the tongue can no man tame; it is an unruly evil, full of deadly poison."

Below I will only use certain clauses of this verse to give light to the thought:

Verse 6:and setteth on fire the course of nature;

When we open our mouths releasing *words* <u>we set in motion</u> a course of action. When *words* are released *Word*Man is born and goes into action in the fulfillment of itself. Here is a great opportunity to become responsible. With this thought in mind, let us begin to speak not just on purpose but with purpose, according to the actions desired.

I remember when I met my wife she released words on my behalf; she said "I would write books." Here today you see her words fulfilled after a course of actions beginning in December of 2009 according to the opening of her mouth setting things in motion for the manifestation of this book.

Here James points out the power of the tongue from another angle. He talks about the horse and the bridle being in the horse's mouth. The bridle sits on the horse's tongue and can turn its whole body in obedience to the person riding it. The rudder is likewise in comparison to the tongue that stirs or direct the ship regardless of its size. A rudder is a primary control surface used to stir a ship. With that thought in mind, there's no problem in your life that's too big for *word* man.

James makes a statement in verse 8.

[8] But the tongue can no man tame;

- *Tame: to make less powerful and easy to control*

When you look at this statement it appears James is telling us that we can't control our tongue. Well it's my tongue and if I wanted to lick the pavement, dirt, or the bottom of my shoe I could. Here James is not talking about the physical aspect of the tongue but the spiritual. Earlier we talked about the power of the tongue in the book of Proverbs identifying that power. James simply tells us that we can't control this power. We as people always say stuff we don't mean, often we try to take back what we say or weaken the blow of it by saying, I'm just playing. This doesn't make it voided or lesser in power, your tongue has just formed a *word* man. **_The word man you released only has one goal in mind, and that is to fulfill itself._** This is what I would call, (authentic) selfishness. This word in Latin or Greek has the same meaning.

Authentic: *GR:Authentikos-*

- Principal
- Genuine

I love the idea of these two words but I would like to only major on the one.

- *Principal: First in order of importance.*

When it comes to *word man* the order of importance is fulfillment. This is the sole purpose of his existence.

Listen to what James is saying in verse 8: *"But the tongue can no man tame;"*

This is what that implies, no other man can decide what happens in your life. When I say life, I'm implying in your home, in your marriage, at your job, or with your children. The Father didn't put our destiny in the power of other people, nor in the shade of your skin, but rather in our mouth. So, put the blame where it really belongs.

Romans 10:8-10 KJV

[8] But what saith it? The word is nigh thee, even in thy mouth, and in thy heart: that is, the word of faith, which we preach; [9] That if thou shalt confess with thy mouth the Lord Jesus, and shalt believe in thine heart that God hath raised him from the dead, thou shalt be saved. [10] For with the heart man believeth unto righteousness; and with the mouth confession is made unto salvation.

Salvation: A source or means of being saved from harm, ruins, or loss.

Our deliverance from every harmful, hurtful, or incriminating thing is in our mouth. This is the thought; ***Our Confessions*** brings us into a place of safety. Our deliverance is closer to us than the fingers on our hands, it is in our mouth. The way out of every situation is in your mouth, because whether we want to admit it or not that is the very reason the situation exists. When I was in a dilemma with being in my daughter life I asked my Pops (Dr. David Oatis) about it and his response to me was, "How did you get in good with the mother of your child before she was born?" I really didn't know what he was looking for as a response so I stalled and then he said, "With your mouth." I then understood that it was my mouth that would get me back in good with her mother that I may be in my daughter life. *Word* is ready to start working to bring everything you say into being. I'm not trying to tell some good story to make this book interesting. This is me agreeing with the WORD OF

GOD that I may help my fellow citizen. I didn't say it, I just agreed with GOD'S WORD.

Listen to this thought:

- Our ignorance of this truth doesn't make it not so.

This is a spiritual insight to how the Kingdom works on behalf of the believing ones. Listen to Jesus in Luke:

See Luke 8:10 MSG

"He said, "You've been given insight into God's kingdom---<u>you know how it works</u>. There are others who need stories. But even with stories some of them aren't going to get it: Their eyes are open but don't see a thing, their ears are open but don't hear a thing."

Here I would like to build my case. Every born-again believer should know how the Kingdom works, for it is given for us to know the mysteries. God gives us His Spirit, and His Word that we may know so we are without excuse.

(YOU KNOW HOW IT WORKS!)

1 Corinthians 2:9-10 KJV , "But as it is written, Eye hath not seen, nor ear heard, neither have entered into the heart of man, the things which God hath prepared for them that love him. [10] But God hath revealed them unto us by his Spirit: for the Spirit searcheth all things, yea, the deep things of God."

Why do the Spirit search all the things of God? To reveal them to us, for they were prepared for us. The Father is not hiding this from His children, but rather making it available to all, free, and unconditionally. I made the following statement in my previous book. ***"LIVING FROM AN ETERNAL STANDPOINT"***

Scripture reference:

John 3:15 KJV "That whosoever believeth in him should not perish, but have eternal life."

Here Jesus helps us in identifying this life. This passage simply says that when a person believes in Jesus he or she receives this life and it also denotes that he or she prior to their act of believing did not have this life. But now in the place of a life that is perishing comes a life of the God kind.

It would be very unfair of the Father to bring us into this way of life but keep us ignorant of how it works. Think about it this way, however things work for the Father is how they work for His children. Let's take a closer look at how the Father get things done.

See Genesis 1:3,6,9,11,14,20,24,26 KJV"

And God said, Let there be light: and there was light. [6] And God said, Let there be a firmament in the midst of the waters, and let it divide the waters from the waters. [9] And God said, Let the waters under the heaven be gathered together unto one place, and let the dry land appear: and it was so. [11] And God said, Let the earth bring forth grass, the herb yielding seed, and the fruit tree yielding fruit after his kind, whose seed is in itself, upon the earth: and it was so. [14] And God said, Let there be lights in the firmament of the heaven to divide the day from the night; and let them be for signs, and for seasons, and for days, and years: [20] And God said, Let the waters bring forth abundantly the moving creature that hath life, and fowl that may fly above the earth in the open firmament of heaven. [24] And God said, Let the earth bring forth the living creature after his kind, cattle, and creeping thing, and beast of the earth after his kind: and it was so. [26] And God said, Let us make man in our image, after our likeness: and let them have dominion over the fish of the sea, and over the fowl of the air, and over the cattle, and over all the earth, and over every creeping thing that creepeth upon the earth."

I chose to take these passages from the stage of creation allowing the reader to see *Word Man* at work for the Father in creation. Here we see clearly when the Father wanted something done He simply said, and as His children we must know that when we say there's a creative force that come forth from our mouth. **I have taken the notion to give it a name. (WORD MAN)**

Two important principles:

- The power of the Kingdom is released through the spoken word.

- Word Man is released in every word that is uttered empowered by the Kingdom.

Also in my book, ***"Living From An Eternal Standpoint"***, I made the following statement on defining what living from an eternal standpoint denotes:

"Living from there would also insinuate that's where I speak from as well. Words, they come out of my mouth but not from my mouth. There needs to be a consciousness of this. *Word* is eternity words are eternal. When we speak, our *word* come from the real us, the eternal being that we are our true self, spirit."

Ecclesiastes 3:11 NLT

[11] Yet God has made everything beautiful for its own time. He has planted eternity in the human heart, but even so, people cannot see the whole scope of God's work from beginning to end.

Here we have it in a nut shell.

1 It's set for a specific time and that time was the coming of Jesus.

2 It was planted in the one and only place that it could be identified, the spirit.

3 It cannot and will not be known or understood from observation in the natural.

Matthew 12:35 AMP

[35] The good man from his inner good treasure flings forth good things, and the evil man out of his inner evil storehouse flings forth evil things.

Words come out of our mouth but from our spirits or hearts. This is what we are, and everything we do, we do from here. When the father wants to get something into the earth he first places a desire in man's heart then man turns and releases these desire out of his mouth in the form of words. Now these words began the process of fulfillment where that desire is concerned. This isn't you just joking around with words this is you speaking from an eternal standpoint.

1 You've taken an eternal stance.

2 You are conscious in your stance

3 You now live, breath, move, and SPEAK according to the stance you've taken.

4 Your words are a product of the stance you've taken.

Here's a thought, when a female conceives it is only because she has received seed. She receives the seed; she incubates that seed until it is fully developed then it comes out of her and though she nurtures it and grows it in her the seed does not come from her. The seed comes from the male!

Isaiah 55:11 KJV

[11] So shall my word be that goeth forth out of my mouth: it shall not return unto me void, but it shall accomplish that which I please, and it shall prosper in the thing whereto I sent it.

- Word is unstoppable
- Word is purposeful
- Word is fail proof

This is a need to know thing, when word is released, assignment is the only thing it longs for. Fulfillment of itself is the only thing that can satisfy the longing of word. When word is on the move it doesn't stop to entertain no one or no thing. Word is seen twice during its life span.

- When it is born
- When it is fulfilled

When word is born into the world it has in it the ability to fulfill its assignment, when it has fulfilled the assigned purpose it no longer has reason to exist.

Word is conceived through the gates of your eyes and ears, It'incubated in the mind, and the mouth is the birth canal in which it enters the earth.

Psalm 107:20 KJV

[20] He sent his word, and healed them, and delivered them from their destructions.

John 1:1 KJV

"In the beginning was the Word, and the Word was with God, and the Word was God."

Here we see that word gets its nature, substance and origin from GOD/WORD. If God thinks that it's important to make word equivalent as Himself then we too must view word in this same light.

James 1:18 KJV

"Of his own will *begat* he us with the word of truth, that we should be a kind of first fruits of his creatures."

- Begat:
  - To procreate, as a father, or to generate; as, to beget a son.

  - To produce, as an effect; to cause to exist; to generate.

This passage clearly points out that we as man is a product of the word, but this is not what this book is about. This is not about the product but the creative force that created the product. Let me point this out while we're in this vain. Because man is a product, and an offspring of the word, that same creative force now works for and on mans behalf every time he opens his mouth. That very same force!

Chapter 3

TEAM WORK

Amos 3:3 KJV

[3] Can two walk together, except they be agreed?

What do I mean when I say team work? We have already discussed what and who Word Man is. Let's just recap, he, (Word Man) is our words coming out of our mouth taking on the form of an unseen man with one goal in mind and that is the fulfillment of itself.

Team work is when we believe the Word of God and in our believing we take sides with God for the enrichment of our lives according to His will, purpose, and plan for us. We simply agree with God making the things He say the things we say, its then when Word Man springs forth from our mouth and team up with the Word of God on our behalf. Now the power of God's Word coupled with the power of our words works as a team on, in, and through our lives.

Matthew 18:19 KJV

[19] Again I say unto you, That if two of you shall agree on earth as touching anything that they shall ask, it shall be done for them of my Father which is in heaven.

I was born at J.P.S.(John Peter Smith) hospital in Fort Worth Texas. My mother gave birth to twin boys, Percy and Perry Petite. As you know, the doctor has to do an overall health inspection.

Well, once it was all done they came baring the bad news, they told her the younger one has asthma. Well as they went through the proper talk concerning the diagnosis my mother agreed with the doctors words simply by saying ok.

I would like to point out that it was then when this passage was at work in my life.

Matthew 18:19 "That if two of you shall agree on earth as touching anything that they shall ask, it shall be done."

Now after this she would keep the agreement renewed day after day month after month year after year by rehearsing the words of the doctor. She would not let me play with the other kids when they played ruff she would always say to me, boy don't be out there playing ruff you know you got asthma.

When I was about six years old we went to a healing crusade and after the preacher was done preaching he gave an alter call for all who was sick and wanted to be healed. My mother took me up to be prayed for. I remember just as clear when he finished praying he said to me God has healed you from asthma. Years after that I still suffered with asthma. Once we got home it looked like I wouldn't deal with this thing anymore. The very next day my mother renewed her contract with the devil;oh I mean the doctor. How? You might ask.

- First, she never agreed with the preacher.
- Second, the very next day she rehearsed what seemed to be her favorite words. Boy don't be out there playing ruff you know you got asthma.

Now because of that I remember being in and out the hospital wrestling with these words that where working together to keep bound with this devil called asthma.

Year of 1993 eighteen years of age I was struck really hard by this demonic sickness called asthma It was so bad the doctor said that if I would not have came in when I did I would have died. They admitted me in that night and treated the symptoms. I was released two days later, I remember the tunting words of the doctor playing over and over in my mind as I walked home. Happy to be out of the hospital and alive I skip all the way.

John 14:26 KJV

[26] But the Comforter, which is the Holy Ghost, whom the Father will send in my name, he shall teach you all things, and bring all things to your remembrance, whatsoever I have said unto you.

While I was walking home this voice began to speak to me, I was also reminded of the time when my mother took me to the healing crusade and the words of that preacher came up ringing in my spirit.

(God has healed you from asthma.)

I remember it like it was yesterday, I stop, and as I pondered on this, I knew in my heart what it meant and so I just began to say out loud with my own mouth. I don't have asthma, God healed me. It was then I began to run as I continued to say, I don't have asthma, God healed me.

I couldn't wait to get home to tell my family. I believe it was then I preached my first massage of Gods ability to heal. And I have been rehearsing that story every since that time. I now know that voice to be the voice of the Holy Spirit and I've been in agreement with the preacher, the Word of God, and the Holy Spirit every since. I'm forty years of age now and still free from asthma. Glory to God!

Chapter 4

BE SLOW TO SPEAK

James 1:19-20 KJV

[19] Wherefore, my beloved brethren, let every man be swift to hear, slow to speak, slow to wrath: [20] For the wrath of man worketh not the righteousness of God.

The book of James is known for its out look on how we are to take into consideration the mouth. Let's look at what he has to say with this thought in mind, be slow to speak. Here we see he uses the word slow in two clauses of this verse.

A-Clauses: slow to speak

B-Clause: slow to wrath

When a person becomes angry they aren't thinking about the words that are coming out of their mouth, the mouth is the one way we as the children of God pleases our Father with words of faith. This is also true in the natural as well in the spirit. According to Hebrews 11:6 without faith it is impossible to please the Father. listen to this passage.

2 Corinthians 4:13 KJV

[13] We having the same spirit of faith, according as it is written, I believed, and therefore have I spoken; we also believe, and therefore speak;

The thought is this; with this new life that we now live, we live to please the Father looking, thinking, acting, and speaking like Him. The life we live is a life of faith therefore the words we speak are words of faith. This you will not and can not do in the wrath of man only the faith of God. This is why He gave us His Son, His Word, an His Spirit.

My wife sometimes wonders why I don't talk a lot, she would sometimes get upset with me and no matter what she would say to try and get me to say something, I just sat there, truth is, I was just as upset as she was. And it would make her even mad the more when I didn't respond. This is what I understood, if I wanted this conversation to die then I needed to keep my mouth shut.

We are still talking about the power of words. We must learn to be slow to speak, or we will wreck havoc in or own lives.

1 Peter 3:10 KJV

[10] For he that will love life, and see good days, let him refrain his tongue from evil, and his lips that they speak no guile:

- Guile
- Sly or cunning intelligence

Have you ever spoke to someone that was trying to conn you out of something? This is what you call, **_(word abuse.)_** The word **abuse** derives from two words in our English dictionary fused together, abnormal and uses. Let's look at this words by way of definition .

- **Abnormal:**

- Deviating from what is normal or usual.
- When something is used for a purpose in which it was not created or intended.

- **Uses**

- Take, hold, or deploy something as a means of accomplishing a purpose or achieving a result.

People have been committing the act of abuse with words for years. This is a result of one or two things, unconsciousness or ignorance.

- **Unconsciousness:**
  - The state of being uninformed or unaware.

You cannot be aware of that in which you have not been informed.

Notice, sometimes people do things and when they come to themselves they say, what have I done? This is an act of unconsciousness; this person did the thing unconsciously. When one unconsciously commit an act, they can't recall what they did, but they see the results. This is the same with words. When one speaks, opening his or her mouth releasing the power of the tongue in the form of words people end up hurt as a result.

The earth is full of believers, though many of them are unconscious. Many believe are unaware of who they are, where they come from, why they exist, what they can do, and where they are going. There can be no true fulfillment in life because they haven't been informed, therefore rendering them helpless, because of their ignorance they continue to use words abnormally. Let's not continue in ignorance, but rather let us speak on purpose and with purpose!

Chapter 5

WORD AND FLESH

John 1:14 KJV

[14] And the Word was made flesh, and dwelt among us, (and we beheld his glory, the glory as of the only begotten of the Father,) full of grace and truth.

Look closely at this passage. The Word was made flesh but never stop being The Word. Word has the ability to take on other forms in pursuit of the fulfillment of itself. Here's a thought, when we open our mouths and release words, these words will come to pass.

I was talking to a few people one day standing over a stove as smoke neck bones were simmering in a pot. I opened my mouth and said that I would like some hot sauce seeing that there was none in the house, as we continued and on talking about other things I didn't think nothing of the hot sauce no more after that day. I went on about life as normal, after a couples of days past by I walked into the house where I was living at the time and one of the people I was talking to the other day was there and had gotten me a bottle of Louisiana Hot Sauce. She said, I was walking through the store and I remembered what you said about hot sauce. Well what did I say? *It was at that moment this revelation was demonstrated. My words had become my reality.*

- WHAT I SEE IS NOT MY REALITY, WHAT I SAY BECOMES MY REALITY. ~DR, DAVID OATIS PSY.D

- WHEN I OPEN MY MOUTH I AM CALLING FOR THE VERY THING I SAY. ~DR, DAVID OATIS PSY.D

Word has no limitation we see word walk through 42 generations and shows up in the manifested form of Jesus Christ. *Word transcends generations we don't have to wait for our great great grand kids to show up before we speak a word on their behalf.* The Father sent His word to heal and deliver us long before we were even thought of by our parents. Just like the Father's word walked through generation after generation and manifested itself in the form of Jesus, let us speak words of heath and deliverance for our generations. For me, the word showed up wearing the name Dr. David Oatis. We are products of The Word in a flesh body, we are not the body, we are in the body, therefore while at home in the body we are able to partner with word on the behalf of its fulfillment.

Chapter 6

WORD AND SPIRIT

John 6:63 KJV

"It is the spirit that quickeneth; the flesh profiteth nothing: the words that I speak unto you, they are spirit, and they are life."

- **Quickeneth:**
  - Spring to life.
  - Give or restore life.

Our words have the ability to give and restore life. Spoken words are life giving spirits, causing life to spring forth. they have the ability and will bring forth the thing you say giving life to it. Word is the very fabric of our being and it would stand the reason we need to know and understand words.

- **Three things you need to know**
- What is word?
- Word is the one thing by which all things exist.

- Why is word?
- Word is the founding process of getting things done spiritually.

- How does it work?
- With the mouth by the power of the tongue.

YOU CALL FOR THE VERY THING YOU SAY

Isaiah 55:10-11 KJV

[10] "For as the rain cometh down, and the snow from heaven, and returneth not thither, but watereth the earth, and maketh it bring forth and bud, that it may give seed to the sower, and bread to the eater: [11] So shall my word be that goeth forth out of my mouth: it shall not return unto me void, but it shall accomplish that which I please, and it shall prosper in the thing whereto I sent it."

Many of times we wonder why stuff shows up in our life, what we don't understand is how it gets there. Our words work for us, as we see in Isaiah what we say will return to us and it isn't returning empty handed. I made a statement earlier in a previous chapter, "Don't just speak on purpose but rather with purpose." Our lives must become our targets, with our words being the arrows in which we use to aim for the mark of the life we desire. We have this saying; "Loose lips sink ships." This is a fact and it is confirmed in The Word of God.

Proverbs 6:2 KJV

[2] "Thou art snared with the words of thy mouth, thou art taken with the words of thy mouth."

Good or bad; our words are working to bring into our life the very things we say. Don't get caught up with the thought of your mouth has gotten you into a mess. This is the thought, the same way things show up in your life is the same way they will leave, with YOUR mouth.

A few years ago I worked in a processing plant and everybody there knew me to be a minster so they would call me Rev. A young man would come to me every night for advice about his relationship. All he would say to me was the things he thought were bad! He never seemed to have any good thing to say about the relationship. You will not be able to help people like this; you can't until they are willing to say something different. I shared with this fellow from the scripture that his words are seeds and his relationship was the ground in which they were sown and if he was going to get anything good from that ground he would have to change what he's been saying. You can't sow apples seeds expecting an orange tree, you must sow for what you want. One night led by the Spirit I said to the young man, "If you can't say anything good to me from now on about your relationship don't talk to me no more about it." Sad to say he never talk to me anymore about it.

This isn't just some saying, it's a spiritual principle! And just like gravity when you drop something it automatically falls to the ground, it sets in motion a course of action every time you open your mouth.

Galatians 6:7-8 KJV

[7] "Be not deceived; God is not mocked: for whatsoever a man soweth, that shall he also reap. [8] For he that soweth to his flesh shall of the flesh reap corruption; but he that soweth to the Spirit shall of the Spirit reap life everlasting."

Mark 4:14 KJV

[14] "The sower soweth the word."

Even as a seed produces after what it's called even so words produce according to what is said. Watermelon seed produces watermelon. The life of the seed is in itself. The ability of the seed to produce what it is called is self- fulfilling.

There are two principles that apply here.
1. The power of the Kingdom is release through the spoken word.
2. The Ambassador speaks with the of the authority of the King.

I once led the outreach ministry for our church- Heavenly H.O.P.E. Ministries and I would go downtown with a group of ministers to help in feeding those that were homeless. It was also a team of ministries that went every Sunday. The Lord placed the burden on my heart to continue in assisting the ministry which started the outreach and so my wife and I committed to assist the ministry as our own. We called it the homeless ministry. Let me make a statement here: "A thing will only produce after what it is called." The Lord quickened my heart on this thought. One day as I mediated on the ministry thinking about how to bring change to the lives that we would encounter, I saw the problem. We continued to call it one thing expecting it to produce something else. That was it! We needed to change the name of the ministry. This thought burned in my heart as I awaited the chance to share this with my family and the other ministers that served alongside of me. We never called it the homeless ministry again and immediately change began to manifest. Every week after that someone would come and give a testimony of how they were restored back with their family, others got jobs, and begin to be able to rent homes, and pay bills. All this begin to happen just at the rewording of the name of a ministry. This is Word Man in action!!!! Glory to God!!!!

This picture give a clear identity to word man. Word man is doing the very thing he was sent to do and he will not stop until he is fulfilled in that which he was sent out to do. My pops Dr. David OatisPsy.Donce said to me, *"He's a word God, it's a word world, and we are word rulers."*

We must see the ability of words and learn how to put them to use for the greater good.

Last Remarks

In closing, abusive tendencies in relationships starts with the way we think of ourselves and our significant other forming words that are death to our relationship. To stop abuse in relationships we must change the way we think which will change the way we say and what we say. The tone of voice you use with someone can start an argument not just what you say to them. Society must grasp that verbal abuse is just as bad as physical because it leaves emotional scars that can last a life time consciously or unconsciously.

R.E.V.I.V.E. seeks to stop this repeated cycle of abuse. We strive to educate society on the different forms of abuse and heal or prevent it with the Word of God. We pray that this book helps you identify the abusive tendencies that you need to change and be able to recognize when someone is abusing you. We pray that this book helps you to understand that your words are life or death and you must develop your relationship with God so you can become more conscious of what words you release in the supernatural world that you live in. We pray that you read this book over and over until you become an individual that understands that you have power to manifest God's word with the words that you say. The Bible states in Mark 11:23 :"For verily I say unto you, That whosoever shall say unto this mountain, Be thou removed , and be thou cast into the sea; and shall not doubt in his heart, but shall believe that those things which he saith shall come to pass; he shall have WHATSOEVER HE SAITH." This was Jesus talking to the body of

Christ and he was telling us we have whatever we say....GOOD OR BAD. So we pray that we watch the words we release in relationships, over our relationships, and in our life in general.

If you need help with understanding more about abuse; feel free to contact us today.

Here is some more important information that will help you on your journey to emotional healing in your relationship:

Domestic Violence and **Emotional Abuse** are behaviors used by one person in a relationship to control the other. Partners may be married or not married; heterosexual, gay, or lesbian; living together, separated or dating.

Examples of Abuse include:
* *Name-calling or putdowns*
* *Keeping a partner from contacting their family or friends*
* *Withholding money*
* *Stopping a partner from getting or keeping a job*
* *Actual or threatened physical harm*
* *Sexual assault*
* *Stalking*
* *Intimidation*

Violence can be criminal and includes physical assault (hitting, pushing, shoving, etc.), sexual abuse (unwanted or forced sexual activity), and stalking. Although emotional, psychological, and financial abuse is not criminal behavior; they are forms of abuse and can lead to criminal violence.

Abuse takes many forms and can happen all the time or once in a while. An important step to help yourself or someone you know in preventing or stopping abuse is recognizing the warning signs listed on the *"Violence Wheel."* **ANYONE CAN BE A VICTIM!** Victims can be of any age, sex, race, culture, religion, education, employment or marital status. Although both men and women can be abused, most victims are women.

Children in homes where there is domestic violence are more likely to be abused and/or neglected. Most children in these homes know about the violence. Even if a child is not physically harmed, they may have emotional and behavior problems.

If you are being abused, remember:
    1. You are not alone.
    2. It is not your fault.
    3. Help is available.

Love Is Respect
The National Teen Dating Abuse Helpline: 1-866-331-9474 or TTY 1-866-331-8453, text "Loveis" to 22522 or live chat at **loveisrespect.org**

Call the U.S. National Sexual Assault Hotline

#WORDMAN   Dr.(s) Perry and Shay Petite

1-800-656-HOPE (4673)
Secure, online private chat is available at
https://ohl.rainn.org/online/

Domestic Violence Wears Many Tags
On Facebook as *Domestic Violence Wears Many Tags Organization*
202-821-8933

IRIS
Domestic Violence Center
Capital Area 24 hour Crisis Line
225-389-3001 or 1-800-541-9706
www.stopdv.org

This chart is a way of looking at the behaviors abusers use to get and keep control in their relationships

Battering is a choice. It is used to gain power and control over another person. Physical abuse is only one part of a system of abusive behaviors. Do you see any of the behaviors on the wheel in how you interact with others? This physical abuse leads to other forms of abuse.

Each part shows a way to control or gain power.
ABUSE IS NEVER A ONE TIME EVENT.

According to the FBI, a woman is battered every 15 seconds.

POWER AND CONTROL WHEEL

PHYSICAL VIOLENCE SEXUAL

- **USING COERCION AND THREATS**: Making and/or carrying out threats to do something to hurt her/him • threatening to leave her/him, to commit suicide, to report her/him to welfare • making her/him drop charges • making her/him do illegal things
- **USING INTIMIDATION**: Making her/him afraid by using looks, actions, gestures • smashing things • destroying her/his property • abusing pets • displaying weapons
- **USING EMOTIONAL ABUSE**: Putting her/him down • making her/himfeel bad about herself/himself • calling her/him names • making her/him think she's/he's crazy • playing mind games • humiliating her/him • making her feel guilty
- **USING ISOLATION**: Controlling what she/he does, who she/he see and talks to, what she/he reads, where she/he goes • limiting her/his outside involvement • using jealousy to justify actions
- **MINIMIZING, DENYING AND BLAMING**: Making light of the abuse and not taking her/his concerns about it seriously • saying the abuse didn't happen • shifting responsibility for abusive behavior • saying she/he caused it
- **USING CHILDREN**: Making her/him feel guilty about the children • using the children to relay messages • using visitation to harass her/him • threatening to take the children away
- **USING MALE PRIVILEGE**: Treating her/him like a servant • making all the big decisions • acting like the "master of the castle" • being the one to define men's and women's roles
- **USING ECONOMIC ABUSE**: Preventing her/him from getting or keeping a job • making her/him ask for money • giving her/him an allowance • taking her/his money • not letting her/him know about or have access to family income

PHYSICAL VIOLENCE SEXUAL

* Louisiana ranks 2nd in the nation for homicides related to domestic abuse.
* 2-4 million American women are abused each year.
* White, Black, Hispanic & Non-Hispanic women have equivalent rates of violence committed by intimate partners.
* Nearly 1/2 of men who abuse their female partners, also abuse their children.
* Up to 50% of homeless women and children in this country are fleeing domestic violence.

* Studies show that women face the greatest risk of assault when they leave or threaten to leave their partners, or report the abuse to authorities.

R.E.V.I.V.E.

Reaching Excellent Victorious Innocent Victims Equally

IF you have any questions or need any service in understanding what you are facing contact us today at 318-719-0212 or by email shawanda.petite@gmail.com. **Our mission is to raise awareness of domestic violence through advocacy, conferences, workshops, counseling, songs, and every opportunity that can be seized.**

#IOVERCAME
Revived to Set the Captives Free

Made in the USA
Coppell, TX
28 February 2022

74204705R00050